Original title:
Twilight in the Tall Timbers

Copyright © 2025 Creative Arts Management OÜ
All rights reserved.

Author: Milo Harrington
ISBN HARDBACK: 978-1-80567-397-2
ISBN PAPERBACK: 978-1-80567-696-6

The Nestle of Night Among Branches

As day bids farewell with a cheeky wink,
The squirrels gather, their gossip in sync.
With acorns as crowns, they strut and they chatter,
While chipmunks roll by, looking none the fatter.

The owls play poker, a hoot and a croak,
With wisecracks and puns, they shimmer and poke.
While the bats polish shades, flapping with flair,
Pretending to pose for a night-time affair.

Frogs croon ballads, a croaky rock band,
Ribbiting rhythms, a crazy night planned.
The fireflies dance, in their flickering suits,
They twirl in formation, the tiniest hoots.

A rabbit named Dave tells jokes till he's hoarse,
While the deer stand by, rolling eyes of remorse.
They snicker and snort, in their woodland delight,
As the stars peek through, adding punch to the night.

The Stillness Before the Dark

In woods where shadows twist and sway,
The critters whisper, 'Dance, hooray!'
A squirrel juggles acorns high,
As raccoons plot a food supply.

The branches creak, the leaves all rustle,
While owls don capes, prepare for tussle.
The moon peeks out, a sneaky sprite,
And bats wear masks for comic fright.

A Haven When the Light Grows Dim

When daylight dims, the fireflies wink,
The frogs begin their croaky sync.
A hedgehog twirls a dapper dance,
While crickets form a merry prance.

The trees all giggle, branches sway,
'Time for a laugh, it's end of day!'
The stars come out, they cheer and sing,
As night wraps up its cozy fling.

Lighthouse of Shadows in the Timberland

Amid the pines, a glow so bright,
A lantern's glow, oh what a sight!
The raccoons gather, hats askew,
To hold a party just for you.

With donuts made from moss and glee,
They toast to shadows, wild and free.
A deer attempts a clumsy jig,
While owls hoot loud, 'Now dance, you big!'

Embracing Nightfall in the Grove

As the sun dips low, the trees all grin,
A fox pulls up to join the din.
With twinkles bright, they raise a cheer,
For nighttime fun is finally here!

The shadows play their silly games,
While beetles rustle and move like flames.
The night unfolds, a tapestry,
Of laughter, light, and pure esprit.

Solstice Serenade in the Tree Heights

In branches high with squirrels at play,
The sun bows low, a bright ballet.
A chipmunk grins, a joke in hand,
While the woodpecker taps—a rock band.

The breeze whispers secrets, a playful tease,
While shadows dance with exceptional ease.
A raccoon winks, wearing a hat,
As the owl hoots, 'Who's up for a chat?'

Mysterious Echoes of Dimly Lit Glades

A shadowy figure makes a bizarre sound,
Is it a deer or a lost hound?
The bushes rustle, a leaf takes flight,
A tangle of gnomes planning all night.

Beneath the stars that twinkle with glee,
The frogs croak tales of what they see.
Mice hold a dance under a mushroom cap,
As the owls complain, 'We're missing the map!'

The Last Glow of Day Among Giants

As the sun dips low with a yawn and a stretch,
The trees gossip, 'Bet we're the best-pitched!'
A deer in a bow tie, quite debonair,
While a turtle spins tales with nary a care.

With laughter echoing through leafy hallways,
Creatures gather, avoiding the sun's rays.
A raccoon stumbles, trips over a root,
Waving goodbye in his slick little suit.

Beneath the Velvet Sky of Pines

In the cool of the dusk, where shadows sway,
A hedgehog sings, 'What a bright end of day!'
Pine cones giggle, rolling around,
While fireflies compete, lighting the ground.

From a branch above, a squirrel looks down,
Saying, 'Why so serious? Let's paint this town!'
With acorns as hats, they throw a grand ball,
As crickets chirp, 'Join or you'll fall!'

Secrets of the Gloaming Woodlands

In the hush of evening's grace,
Squirrels dance, but have no place.
With acorns flying through the air,
They giggle loud without a care.

A raccoon sneaks in for a snack,
Stealing treats from the woodland pack.
He wears a mask, but that's no crime,
Just a thief passing his time.

Fireflies flash like tiny stars,
Guiding lovers, or perhaps cars.
"Watch your step, don't trip and fall!"
Echoes bounce off each leafy wall.

As shadows stretch with playful might,
Forest creatures weave through the night.
Whispers say they're up to no good,
Laughter erupts in the quiet wood.

The Lullaby of Ferns and Pines

Underneath the ferns so green,
Snoozing critters yet unseen.
A hedgehog rolls, a fox takes flight,
Chasing dreams in pure delight.

The owls hoot a silly song,
Who can guess what's right or wrong?
In the trees, the squirrels rave,
Playing tag, oh, what a wave!

At dusk, raccoons steal the show,
With a dance that's quite the glow.
They spin and twirl, the night's delight,
As shadows twinkle with delight.

So listen close, dear woodland friend,
As silly songs and puns suspend.
At night, the forest comes alive,
In giggles sweet, all trees survive.

Where the Sun Meets the Sylvan Edge

As the sun dips low, they gather near,
Chattering critters, full of cheer.
The frogs croak jokes, the rabbits laugh,
Finding fun in the evening's half.

Bees buzz about, they're on a spree,
Painting flowers, won't you see?
They stumble, trip, then dance away,
Gardens bloom, come out to play.

A deer prances with flair and grace,
Until it slips, oh what a face!
The squirrels share their nightly snack,
"We promise not to hold back!"

So raise a toast to forest nights,
Where laughter dances, and joy ignites.
The sun may set, but bright it seems,
In woodlands deep, the fun redeems.

Veils of Mist in the Dusk-hued Woods

In misty realms where shadows creep,
The critters plot their secrets deep.
A rabbit hops, a secret shared,
As laughter breaks, unprepared.

The nightingale hums a funny tune,
Waking the pines and the moon.
Dance along the forest floor,
With twirls and spins, laugh some more!

A raccoon juggles acorns high,
He's caught a bug flying by!
With silly attempts and cheeky charms,
He's the star of the evening's balms.

So linger here in dusk's embrace,
Where giggles chase the joy of space.
In veils of mist, let laughter grow,
For woodland wonders steal the show.

Embracing the Night Among the Mighty Trees

The trees stand tall, with bark like armor,
They whisper secrets, no one will harm her.
Squirrels conspire, plotting their schemes,
While owls wear glasses and toast with their beams.

The mushrooms giggle as shadows do dance,
In the moonlight's glow, they take a chance.
A fox in a tux, with a bowtie so neat,
Claims he's the king of this forest retreat.

The raccoons are hosting a late-night bash,
With acorns and berries, they'll dine in a flash.
The night air is vibrant, filled with delight,
As creatures of charm make the darkness so bright.

Hushed Murmurs in the Dimming Woods

In the fading light, the whispers begin,
A crow's gossiping about the bear's win.
The trees are eavesdropping, roots intertwined,
While grinning hedgehogs share tales of the blind.

The crickets play cards, their stakes are quite high,
Four-leaf clovers examined with a sly eye.
A raccoon on stilts, what a sight to behold,
Declares his odd dreams of a life made of gold.

A family of owls, they hoot with delight,
Standing guard by the moon, all cozy and tight.
Chirps turn to chuckles, and laughter's the tone,
As shadows enshroud this peculiar throne.

The Gathering Musk of Evening's Breath

The scent of damp earth mingles with cheer,
As fireflies waltz, holding hands without fear.
Mice in their waistcoats scoff at the night,
While the breeze plays the flute, making all things feel right.

A porcupine juggles, oh what a great show,
As laughter erupts from the willows below.
The elders debate where the pine nuts are found,
While chipmunks sneak snacks, oh the joy they surround.

The moon's a big pie, divided for all,
As everyone gathers, waiting for nightfall.
With giggles and frolics, their spirits unite,
In this curious gathering, all's merry tonight.

Serene Shadows in the Heart of the Forest

The shadows grow long, with giggles and games,
While critters are calling each other by names.
A bear brings a cake, it's messy but sweet,
As hedgehogs are bouncing on mushrooms, what a feat!

With a bear on the beat, and a rabbit on keys,
The night fills with melody, carried by breeze.
The rocks tap their feet, in rhythm and rhyme,
As creatures of nighttime all dance out of time.

A deer takes a bow, quite proud of their style,
While twinkling stars smile, shining down with a wile.
With joy rising up through the roots and the leaves,
The forest erupts in what everyone believes.

A Nightfall Mosaic of Nature's Brush

The squirrels wear tiny pajamas,
As night slips on with each little breeze.
Owls hoot like they're telling old dramas,
While raccoons plot heists with great ease.

Fireflies dance in a flickering trance,
While shadows play hide and seek near the brook.
The foxes toss each other a glance,
Like secret agents in a mystery book.

Bats swoop down with an acrobatic flair,
As crickets begin their merry loud song.
The trees share secrets with whispers of air,
While frogs hop along where they all belong.

In the canvas of dusk, nature's in jest,
With laughter echoing all through the glade.
Each critter and creature feels truly blessed,
As night drapes the forest like a grand parade.

The Hush of the Woodland Nook

The trees have a chuckle, shaking their leaves,
As raccoons giggle at squirrels in flight.
Bunnies hop close, with big tricks up their sleeves,
And owls turn their heads, like they're in on the light.

Crickets play symphonies, stars twinkle near,
While shadows tiptoe on the carpet of moss.
A squirrel in a hat offers up a cheer,
And lizards look on, pretending they're boss.

The air is a comedy show with no end,
As badgers jive with the light of the moon.
Each night's a party, with laughter to lend,
In the big, leafy nook where the critters commune.

The gentle hush holds a giggly delight,
As everyone plays the silliest role.
In the stillness of dusk, it feels just right,
For nature's own jesters are stealing the whole.

Under the Gaze of the Watchful Moon

The moon winks down like a playful friend,
While shadows grow tall with a silvery sheen.
Frogs croak their jokes, what a night to spend,
As bats have a feast on the bugs in between.

A chipmunk's grin is a sight to behold,
Wearing a crown made of twigs and clover.
The night is a canvas, bursting with gold,
As laughter floats high, it can't get any lower.

Badgers play poker beneath leafy canopies,
And owls serve drinks from a twig-shaped bar.
While raccoons gossip in their cheeky degrees,
This woodland soirée is the best by far.

The cloak of night hums a funny refrain,
As critters unite in their raucous delight.
With mischief and joy in the heart of the plain,
Under the moon's watch, they party till light.

The Soft Whisper of Evening Air

The breeze tickles leaves with a gentle tease,
While fireflies shimmer in a dance so bright.
Bunnies in top hats begin to freeze,
As shadows stretch out in the soft summer light.

Chirping crickets launch their stand-up routine,
With beetles as fans, cheering every quip.
A raccoon's got jokes that are hardly routine,
While frogs gather round for a snippet of wit.

The high fives exchanged by the owls at play,
Sound like soft laughter that fills up the trees.
As whispers of evening sway worries away,
Each critter finds joy in the cool, calming breeze.

With the air thick with giggles and bright moonlit flair,
The forest is clothed in a whimsical dream.
In the hush of the night, life feels quite rare,
As laughter and fun are the soul's greatest theme.

The Permanent Embrace of Dusk's Glow

In the woods where shadows play,
Squirrels dance in disarray.
Owls hoot with a cheeky grin,
While crickets tune their night-time din.

The raccoon wears a mask so fine,
Thinking he's the star of prime.
Underneath the starry dome,
All the critters feel at home.

A deer prances with fruitcake dreams,
Chasing after wayward beams.
Fireflies glow like tiny jokes,
Lighting up the laughing folks.

As dusk falls, they join the fun,
Beneath the glow of setting sun.
With giggles in the evening air,
Nighttime antics everywhere!

Luminous Pathways Through the Woodland Mist

Through the mist, we waddle slow,
Chasing shadows, don't you know?
Bunnies hop in awkward styles,
Turning deep into the smiles.

The owls throw a grand old bash,
Fuzzy hedgehogs join the splash.
With twinkling eyes, they prance and race,
Each woodland critter finds its place.

Glittering trails made of laughter,
Find the woodpecker's next disaster.
Even trees seem to lean and sway,
As the forest joins the play.

In the coolness, joy ignites,
With the moon as their spotlight.
From fumble to frolic, all partake,
In this misty, merry make!

Echoes of the Setting Sun in the Pines

As the sun dips with a wink,
Chipmunks giggle, birds all blink.
Foxes trade their crafty tricks,
While sunsets tease with rosy kicks.

With every echo, laughter rings,
Silly songs the crickets sing.
Each pines whispers a tale or two,
Sharing chuckles, old and new.

A turtle watches with a sigh,
As squirrels argue who can fly.
The firewood puffs, a smoky jest,
"Who's got the best log?" it asked the rest.

And as night falls with a cheer,
The forest makes it crystal clear:
In this moment, joy will reign,
For echoes dance like sweet champagne!

The Forest's Breath as Night Descends

With a sigh, the forest breathes,
Waves of chuckles in the leaves.
Bears twirl in their nadir dance,
While raccoons join in a prance.

The fawns leap over shadow lines,
While owls plot their night-time fines.
A skunk declares a perfume fight,
"Who's the best at the scent delight?"

As branches rustle, secrets spill,
Mice debating who's best at chill.
Bats swoop down in playful jest,
Chasing their shadows with zest.

Night descends with laughter's glow,
In the woods where stories flow.
With creatures bold and spirits free,
The forest beams in glee!

A Canvas of Crickets and Stars

In the dusk the crickets sing,
Their chatter is quite a funny thing.
The trees sway to the silly beat,
While squirrels dance on tiny feet.

The fireflies spark like tiny jokes,
As owls hoot, the night provoke.
Beneath the branches, laughter flows,
In nature's comedy, who knows?

The raccoons wear their masks so bright,
Sneaking snacks 'til the morning light.
Chasing shadows, they start to prance,
As stars above begin to dance.

With each chirp, the night grows fun,
Nature's symphony has just begun.
In this wild play, we laugh away,
At the antics 'neath the Milky Way.

The Forest's Embrace at Day's End

When the sun begins to wave goodbye,
And the birds settle, no longer fly.
The trees whisper secrets and cheer,
As critters gather, all drawing near.

A deer trips over a tangled vine,
While a bunny hops, feeling divine.
Their antics spark joy through the space,
In this quirky, woodland embrace.

Squirrels sharing their nutty stash,
In a huddle, their jokes come fast.
Beneath a moon, round and bright,
Their laughter echoes through the night.

And as shadows wrap tight and snug,
The forest giggles, a friendly bug.
In this place where odd meets the grand,
Life's laughter dances, hand in hand.

A Tapestry of Stars in the Darkening Sky

As daylight begins to softly fade,
The stars emerge like a playful parade.
Each twinkle's a wink, a funny show,
As night's curtain falls, putting on a glow.

The owls chuckle in their wise way,
While bats swoop in to join the play.
Under the vast, shimmering dome,
The forest feels just like home.

Mice in tuxedos shuffle and squeak,
With moonlit beams lighting up their peek.
In this grand theater, laughter ignites,
As constellations perform through the nights.

The nightingale sings some silly tunes,
While the crickets add in their croons.
Together they weave a tapestry bright,
Of laughter and joy in the starry night.

Rhapsody of Leaves in the Subdued Light

Leaves rustle softly, a giggling sound,
As nature's humor dances around.
Each breeze carries whispers of glee,
In the hush of the woods, it's wild and free.

Bamboo sways like it's having a chat,
While a porcupine jokes with a friendly bat.
Flowers nod in laughter's embrace,
While the trees sport their leafy grace.

The dusk brings a rhapsody sweet,
As creatures all share a comedic feat.
Bushes ripple, and shadows unite,
Creating fun in the fading light.

With whispers and chuckles, the forest thrives,
A symphony of joy for all lives.
Here in this wonder, humor takes flight,
In the subdued glow beneath the night.

The Call of the Owls at Dusk

In the trees, owls start to hoot,
Their eyes like marbles, giving a toot.
Silly squirrels dance on the ground,
Mocking the owls with leaps all around.

The rabbits giggle, looking so spry,
While raccoons plot with a wink in their eye.
"Whooo's on first?" the wise one does ask,
The others chuckle, it's quite the task.

Frisky deer prance with a hop and a skip,
Wondering what the owls might whip.
But all they hear is laughter and hoots,
As the forest joins in, shaking their boots.

Just under the stars, a party ensues,
With creatures around, wearing their best hues.
The call of the owls ignites the night,
With antics so funny, oh what a sight!

Lifting the Veil of the Gathering Night

As the sun dips low, shadows play games,
Critters emerge with ridiculous names.
A possum over there with a hat made of grass,
And a chatty old turtle, in a race — what a gas!

Fireflies blinking, they're having a blast,
Catching the buzzes that help them move fast.
A chorus of croaks from the frogs down below,
As they jump in sync, putting on quite a show.

Leaves whisper secrets, the wind starts to tease,
While ants throw a party, they're down on their knees.
The gathering's lively, a comical sight,
What joy when the stars finally join in the night!

So lift up the veil, let the laughter abound,
In this forest of fun, where silliness is found.
The creatures unite, with mirth as their guide,
Under sky's canvas, they all take pride!

A Symphony Under the Dimmed Stars

Under the dome where the stars play the tune,
Crickets chirp loudly, 'They're late, where's the moon?'
The beats of the night bring a whimsical twist,
As the raccoon prances, waving his fist.

A wildcat purrs, trying to compose,
While a badger hums, lost in his prose.
Bats swoop and dive, in a balletic flight,
Playing tag with the shadows, oh what a sight!

Tree branches sway to the rhythm of fun,
Owls perched high, watching everyone run.
The chorus grows louder, as night stretches on,
Freestyle and silly until the first dawn!

Each note is a giggle, each pause a bright laugh,
Nature's great symphony, no need for a staff.
So revel in sound, let the humor ignite,
In a forest of glee, beneath twinkling light!

The Last Dance of the Ember Clouds

As the sun bids adieu, clouds swirl in delight,
Waltzing with colors, painting the night.
A pink one trips over, lands with a puff,
Makes grumpy gray clouds feel a bit rough.

The moon starts to chuckle from up in the sky,
Watching the clouds as they stutter and fly.
A polka of shadows with a jig and a hop,
While the stars twinkle loudly, 'Oh, never stop!'

Dancing in patterns, with laughter they spin,
The world below watches, with a cheeky grin.
Just like a party where no one is shy,
Embers of joy drift and swirl up high.

So join in the fun as the clouds do their dance,
With whimsy and whim, take part in the chance.
For under the night, every giggle's a cheer,
In a realm where the silly will always endear!

Lullabies of the Looming Oak

In the branches, squirrels prance,
With acorns dancing in their stance.
A sleepy owl hoots a tune,
While raccoons play beneath the moon.

The wind whispers silly tales,
Of hedgehogs in jaunty trails.
A rabbit hops with flair and glee,
While bees buzz tunes like a symphony.

Underneath the oak's embrace,
Laughter echoes, a joyful space.
Fireflies flicker, a glowing choir,
While the shadows play in funny attire.

The night chuckles, stars join in,
As crickets chirp a cheeky grin.
In the lull of this merry place,
Nature sings with a jolly face.

Echoes of Dusk in the Canopy

In the leaves, a giggle sways,
As shadows dance in playful ways.
A porcupine rolls down a hill,
In a fuzzy ball, such a sight to thrill.

The birds squawk jokes, oh what a show,
Each tweet a pun that makes you glow.
Kangaroo mice leap with delight,
As fireflies twinkle in the night.

Beneath the branches, laughter blooms,
While owls count all the forest's rooms.
The pinecones chuckle, what a spree!
As the moon winks down on the glee.

Whispers of the breeze declare,
Foliage shimmies, without a care.
In this canopy of playful cheer,
Nature entertains all who wander near.

Moonlight Kisses the Evergreen

Saplings sway with misty cheer,
As moonbeams tickle without fear.
A lizard struts in a dazzling way,
Singing songs that make you sway.

The pines laugh, their needles gleam,
As crickets spin a funny theme.
Willow trees giggle, a soft ballet,
While owls roll dice for fun at play.

The night unfolds like a comic book,
With raccoons plotting their next hook.
Bark beetles tap, a rhythm tight,
Creating beats in the silver light.

Under stars, in jovial spree,
Nature crafts such comedy.
Laughter bounds from tree to tree,
As the woods host this jubilee.

The Quiet Hour of the Ancient Trees

The ancient trunks in shadows brood,
With whispers of a jovial mood.
A badger trips, stumbles, then leaps,
While the forest giggles and peeps.

The ferns flap like hands in cheer,
As raccoons plan their nightcap beer.
Gnarled roots twist in playful fates,
Chortling softly as fate awaits.

Mossy carpets, plush and bright,
Hold secrets of the frolicsome night.
Beneath each branch, a hearty laugh,
Nature shares its light-hearted half.

As the creatures tease the air,
Echoes of joy float everywhere.
In ancient woods, where stories tease,
Laughter finds a home in trees.

Dance of Fireflies in the Gloom

In the dark they start to twirl,
Flashing lights making me whirl.
Bugs in hats and tiny shoes,
Learning how to dance the blues.

Over the grass they spin with flair,
Glowing raves without a care.
One bumps me, gives a little zap,
Says, "Hey dude, aren't you gonna clap?"

Bouncing high like little stars,
While I trip over garden jars.
Hooray for glee under night's cover,
These little bugs are quite the lovers!

But as I laugh and dance along,
They vanish quick, oh where's my throng?
"Come back, you lights!" I start to plead,
And find my shoes, oh what a deed!

The Sigh of Leaves at Dusk

Leaves gossip softly on the breeze,
Like they've had too much to tease.
Whispering tales of quacks and splats,
Of silly birds and silly bats.

As the day hums its quiet tune,
They shake their heads, "Who needs the moon?"
"Let's plan a party oh so grand,
With acorns, berries, and a cool band!"

"Last week's dance was such a hit,
Did you see the mole who did the split?"
The roots below snicker with glee,
"Oh, let them sparkle, wild and free!"

A rustling burst of cosmic fun,
Leaves grab a partner—yeah, they run!
But when morning calls, they start to hide,
"Shhh, says the breeze, our fun's inside!"

Enchantment of the Evening Shadows

Shadows stretch with a lazy yawn,
Making shapes like a funny fawn.
"Look at me, I'm a fancy bird!"
But then it trips—now how absurd!

As the sun dips with a wink and grin,
The shadows laugh, "Now let's begin!"
Jumping jacks and silly prance,
They twirl below in a wacky dance.

"Quick, someone catch the sneaky light!"
They tumble and roll, what a sight!
"Time for tag under this old tree,
Don't get stuck—run fast and free!"

The moon peeks down, giggling too,
"Shadows, oh shadows, what do you do?"
But they keep playing without a clue,
Under stars that twinkle and woo.

A Canvas of Stars Over Ancient Oaks

Beneath the oaks where wise men meet,
Stars blink down; it's quite the treat.
"Imagine!" one star exclaimed with cheer,
"We're painting here, oh dear, oh dear!"

The oaks roll trunks, puffing up tall,
"Let's host a show, we'll have a ball!"
"Bring the sunflowers, welcome them all,
Watch them prance and spin—oh, what a haul!"

Glittering sprinkles from celestial heights,
The trees sway slow as day turns to night.
The stars start juggling, what a show,
"Catch the bright one!" as they glow.

But oops! They fumble, falling down,
Landing on leaves, making a sound.
"Who invited clumsiness to the play?
Let's blame the wind—oh, what a fray!"

Dance of the Fireflies in the Glade

Little sparks of yellow light,
They zoom and twist in slow delight.
Bouncing high, then low, they drift,
While crickets chirp, their voices lift.

A beetle joins the charming dance,
With two left feet, he takes a chance.
He trips on leaves, and oh, what fun!
The fireflies giggle—oh, what a pun!

Glow worms watch with envy wide,
Yet bop along, they won't abide.
With each small flicker, laughter rolls,
In this bizarre ballet of souls.

As darkness deepens, all unite,
A shining flash, a funny sight.
A nighttime show of silly lights,
Where nature laughs and joy ignites.

Beneath the Boughs of the Whispering Pines

Beneath the boughs, where secrets dwell,
A squirrel whispers, 'All is well!'
A crow starts cawing, cracks a joke,
While acorns drop with just a poke.

A raccoon struts with prideful flair,
His furry tail a wild affair.
Pine needles laugh as they tumble down,
Creating a carpet—nature's gown.

A chipmunk tries a dance routine,
But slides on pine cones, oh so keen!
He twirls and spins, but then he trips,
While laughter echoes from the lips.

Night cloaks all in a gentle wrap,
The trees chuckle, "What a mishap!"
Yet under stars, the fun's not done,
In our dear woods, each day is fun!

Shadows Weave Through the Mossy Floor

In shadowy dance, the creatures play,
A mouse rehearses in his own way.
As shadows weave through mossy drapes,
   He strikes a pose, the silliest shapes.

Frogs take turns doing their croak,
A frog who sings? That's quite a joke!
They leap and splash in muddy glee,
   Waving hello to bumblebees.

A hedgehog rolls, he has a blast,
But trips on roots and tumbles fast!
With giggles ringing through the air,
   Each furry critter without a care.

As dusk descends, the fun won't cease,
Moonlight joins, bringing sweet release.
In harmony, they dance once more,
   Mossy laughter, a forest roar!

The Last Glow in the Heart of the Woods

The last glow flickers, a final jest,
A firefly coughs, 'I need a rest!'
Yet still he winks, 'I'll fly tonight!'
While critters chuckle, what a sight.

As stars emerge, they all convene,
A party starts, the mood's serene.
A raccoon juggles furry friends,
While laughter bubbles, never ends.

Beneath the branches, all entwined,
The creatures share a silly kind.
With shiny eyes, they play and chase,
This glowing night, a warm embrace.

In the heart of woods, they spin and cheer,
Nature's stage filled with good cheer.
As the final flicker bids adieu,
The moonlight grins, for fun anew!

Mossy Retreats at the End of Day

In the woods where the shadows play,
Frogs in tuxedos dance the ballet.
Squirrels plotting who'll steal the show,
While raccoons critique them, "Just so-so!"

Beneath the boughs, a picnic spread,
Mice debate if the cheese is dead.
A bear drops by with a funny quip,
"Who invited the ants? They're all on a trip!"

As the sun dips low, and giggles arise,
Woodpeckers chuckle while acting wise.
"Why did the tree get a haircut today?
It couldn't leave home, it was 'stump-ed' in a way!"

When the crickets begin their strange tune,
Fireflies flash like a cartoonish moon.
As stars emerge, it's a comedic sight,
Nature's laughter lingers in the light.

Conversations Afloat on Silent Streams

A duck and a fish share stories at dusk,
"Who needs a boat? It's better, trust!"
The fish says, "Your quacking's not so grand,
But I'll take your word; it's a fine river band!"

A turtle chimes in, with wisdom to share,
"Why rush through life when you can take air?"
The duck rolls his eyes, "It's not quite that deep,
But your slow-baked tales make me want to sleep!"

"Look at the splash, did you see that bloom?"
A frog leaps by, creating the room.
"I'd award it a ten if it landed just right,
But I'm still locked in this pond, out of flight!"

Clouds drift on by, whispering jokes from above,
While the moon winks down, subtle and suave.
In a realm where the laugh and the chatter weave,
Nature's serenity lets silly dreams believe.

Nature's Peace at the Close of Day

The sun rolls back, its work is done,
With crickets chirping, all join the fun.
A deer trips lightly, slips on a root,
And a wise old owl hoots, "That'll teach you to scoot!"

The breeze brings laughter from far-off trees,
As rabbits gossip with so much ease.
"Did you hear about the dog with a bone?
He dug up the yard and claimed it his own!"

A squirrel rides high on a branch with grace,
Shouting, "Quick! Get the camera, it's my best face!"
But the camera's stuck in a hollowed bark,
"Guess we'll just laugh 'til the dogs bark!"

As the fireflies blink with a flickering cheer,
All of nature gathers, that time of year.
Together they tease under soft fading light,
This peace is a giggle as day turns to night.

An Ode to the Fading Sunbeams

As the sun yawns wide and begins to bend,
Each ray a jester, as daylight friends.
A raccoon with shades lounges in green,
Says, "When it's dark, I'm the night's favorite scene!"

In the distance, a beaver builds up some prank,
With twigs stacked high, it's a grand little tank.
He chuckles aloud, "Just look at my loot!
I'll trump that old otter in a swimsuit!"

Birds gather 'round for an evening of glee,
"I'll whistle a tune, you just follow me!"
While the wind joins in with its playful refrain,
Nature's own concert, a whimsical chain.

As stars peek out, making their intro,
A chorus erupts, "It's time! Let's go!"
On this stage called earth, where laughter survives,
We cheer with the critters, as day starts to dive.

Sighs of the Old Growth Under Moonlight

The trees all gossip, they bend and sway,
As old roots rumble, 'Have you heard today?'
A squirrel's acrobatics, a clumsy display,
The moon chuckles softly, 'What a funny ballet!'

Mossy trunks chuckle, a green joke on bark,
While shadows cavort, like a dance in the dark.
The owls take bets on who'll make a spark,
As crickets bring their chorus, a whimsical lark.

The pines exchange puns, chaos in the air,
A raccoon rolls in, quite without a care.
The stars join the fun, twinkling with flair,
As night tours their kingdom, no tall tale too rare.

So laugh with the trees when the moon draws near,
In this leafy theater, there's nothing to fear.
For even the squirrels take life with good cheer,
While the moon's grand performance is worthy a leer.

The Transition of Day and Night

The sun winks goodbye, a cheeky delight,
While shadows arise, giggling in fright.
The clouds play peek-a-boo, soft and light,
As day bids farewell, what a silly sight!

A bear makes a move, his belly so round,
Stumbling through brambles, he tumbles down sound.
The crickets hold hands, in a circle they're found,
Together they sing, a night-melody bound.

The branches shake hands, a knotty old crew,
Dancing like fools in their leafy debut.
The stars sneak on stage, dressed up in bright blue,
As night slides in smooth, with a flourish or two.

And laughter erupts as the fireflies glow,
Winking at bears who just really don't know,
That tomorrow they'll wake, put on quite the show,
In the playful ballet, where old trees steal the show.

Mystic Journeys Through Leafy Aisles

In the forest of fables, where leaves whisper low,
A banter of branches, a caper on show.
The owls plot mischief, as night begins to grow,
A compass made of laughter, guiding their flow.

The undergrowth giggles, secrets abound,
Where hedgehogs conduct, making quite the sound.
With mushrooms for seats, in a gathering round,
They toast to the stars with a giddy rebound.

A fox with a jest, on stories he thrives,
Ensuring the tales bring the woodland to lives.
As shadows exchange, what a fun way to jive,
Amidst nature's revelry, everyone's alive!

So join in this frolic, let spirits all twirl,
As meadows and valleys embrace a wild whirl.
In this leafy parade, watch giggles unfurl,
For laughter's the magic, in every green swirl.

Sunkissed Pines and Evening Serenades

With a stretch and a yawn, the sun starts to fade,
Pines chuckle and creak, in the softening shade.
The beetles assemble for a ball they've made,
While squirrels, in tuxedos, decide to invade.

The fawns play a game, tag through the thickets,
While rabbits bring snacks—tiny carrot tickets.
Old owls tell tales, full of funny snippets,
As the stars flicker on, as night's bright tickets.

The breezes blow softly, a tune on the air,
Where giggles rise up, traveling without care.
The moon adopts rhythms, a jittery stare,
Yet the whole forest joins in, what a merry affair!

So let's dance with the trees, embrace the night glow,
With fireflies lighting our whimsical show.
For laughter's the treasure, the magic we sow,
Among sunkissed pines, where joy overflows.

Fading Light in the Whispering Thicket

The sun's slipping down, it's losing its chase,
A raccoon in shades took my place.
The owls are hooting, giving a wink,
While the squirrels plot on what to drink.

The fireflies flicker, they dance like fools,
Chasing each other, breaking the rules.
A chipmunk laughs at a bumpy ride,
On a log that's still, but he can't quite hide.

A hedgehog rolls by, wearing a hat,
He looks so dapper, imagine that!
A chorus of crickets join in the fun,
As night settles down, their party's begun.

So here in the thicket, laughter rings clear,
Old trees are gossiping, lending an ear.
The night is alive with chatter and glee,
What a sight in the woods, come laugh with me!

Twilight Tales from the Woodland Breeze

The breeze tells stories of trees with charm,
Whispering secrets, promising no harm.
A fox in a tie juggles acorns around,
While a raccoon claps, tapping the ground.

The moon is peeking, a shy little thing,
As birds in pajamas prepare for a fling.
A bear sips honey, with toast in his paw,
Winks at a deer who's stuck in a straw.

The fireflies bring the glow of delight,
Lighting the path for the critters at night.
With giggles and chuckles, they start to convene,
In this woodland carnival, oh what a scene!

So gather 'round, friends, for stories anew,
Of raccoons and owls, and the adventures they brew.
The night holds a promise of laughter and cheer,
In the breeze of the woods, where we have no fear.

Melodies of the Nightfall Grove

In the grove comes a tune that's hard to resist,
A frog on a lily begins its twist.
The crickets chirp, creating a band,
While a wise old owl conducts with a hand.

A deer drops a beat, with hooves tapping low,
While a squirrel joins in with an acorn show.
The trees sway gently, keeping the time,
As rabbits hop by in a jolly rhyme.

The stars blink above, enjoying the plot,
As the moon hums along, oh what a thought!
With laughter and music, the night feels so bright,
In a world that's thick with joy and delight.

So let's dance with the leaves under this glow,
And sing to the rhythm of friends we all know.
In the nightfall grove, where fun always flows,
We'll cherish the music, wherever it goes!

Reflections of Time in the Forest Deep

In the forest so deep, stories unfold,
Of creatures with quirks and antics so bold.
A porcupine, grinning, wears shoes made of fluff,
While a hedgehog debates if that's cool enough.

The shadows grow longer as laughter takes flight,
A turtle on roller skates glides with delight.
The branches are shaking, that's surely a sign,
That the trees are now dancing, oh how they align!

A rabbit is juggling, clumsy but grand,
With berries and nuts, he's getting a hand.
The fireflies cheer, in their own glowing way,
As nighttime arrives, and the fun's here to stay.

So ponder the time in this forest so bright,
Where laughter echoes and dreams take flight.
With life all around and a silly parade,
In the heart of the woods, let's have fun, unafraid!

The Forest Bows to Night's Approach

The trees wear hats made of stars,
Swaying gently, they giggle from afar.
The critters gather, all fence-sitters,
Making shadow puppets, oh what quitters!

Beneath a sky that's lit with glee,
The squirrels conspire: 'Let's have a spree!
Who can jump highest, touch the moon?
But first, let's feast, it's time for a tune!'

With acorns and berries spread on a mat,
The owls look on, wearing party hats.
"Whooo's ready to dance under this bright glow?"
"Not me!" said the hedgehog, "I'll just roll slow!"

So as the night takes over with grace,
The forest laughs in a playful embrace.
While crickets provide a raucous score,
The trees bow low, inviting more.

The Riddle of Evening in the Grove

What trickery lurks in the fading light?
Is it a dance or a pinecone fight?
The fireflies blink, a game they imply,
'Catch us if you can, or you'll just sigh!'

The robins all chatter, sharing bright tales,
Of beetles and bugs with peculiar trails.
"Did you hear that rumor?" whispers the hare,
"Now the raccoons claim they can fly through the air!"

The branches entwine like pals in a row,
As laughter drifts up; the breeze, it will blow.
Mischief is brewing beneath the soft sky,
As frogs wear bow ties, and ladybugs fly.

So gather 'round, all, let's crack a good joke,
'Raccoons are pilots, or so the trees spoke.'
In the grove where secrets and giggles abound,
The night holds the answers, if only you're found.

Where Time Stands Still Among the Trees

Come join the fun where hours drag slow,
The firs are the guards of this wacky show.
A woodpecker drums a hilariously beat,
While chipmunks flip pancakes, quite the treat!

The shadows play tricks, they dance on the ground,
As leaves whisper secrets, with joy they surround.
"What's next? A parade?" the raccoon chimes in,
"Or hide-and-seek, let the games begin!"

A snail in a tux, oh what a sight,
Says, "Catch me if you can, but take it light!"
While the owls exchange glances, so wise yet so sly,
Counting the times that the fireflies fly.

Time's just a prankster, it bends and it sways,
In this forest of laughter, we'll wish for more days.
So tiptoe and chuckle, let your heart dance free,
For here where we gather, is where we're meant to be.

A Breath Between Day and Dusk

In a pause where the sunlight takes a rest,
The woods wear a cloak of their goofy best.
Bumblebees buzz to a comical tune,
While frogs argue loudly, 'We'll swim to the moon!'

The blushing blooms play hide-and-seek,
They giggle and hide, so sly and sleek.
"Just one more peek!" the daisies all shout,
"This time we'll run, let there be no doubt!"

As the shadows stretch like an old cat's yawn,
The forest is filled with the magic of dawn.
"Nap time!" croaks out a sleepy old crow,
So everything softens in the twilight glow.

But before we sleep, let's have one last laugh,
A partridge does juggling with a glance to the past.
In this blink between moments, we swirl and we sway,
Tomorrow's adventures are just a fun day away!

Guardians of the Evening Sky

In cloaks of mist, the trees all cheer,
Swaying to whispers only they hear.
Branches like arms, they give a wave,
To the squirrels who dance, oh, how they behave!

As stars appear, the critters take flight,
Racoon in a top hat? What a sight!
Owls in bow ties, attending the show,
With jackets of bark, they strut to and fro.

The crickets strike chords with such flair,
While fireflies wink, saying, "We dare!"
Dancing in sync, the night's gala unfolds,
And every tall timber, a story retold.

With laughter and giggles, the forest feels bright,
As shadows play tag in the softening light.
These guardians know how to end the day,
With humor and joy, they guide us away.

Where Shadows Stretch in the Stillness

When the sun dips low, the trees start to grin,
With shadows that dance like they've downed a few gin.
The owls swap jokes as they perch on a branch,
While the leaves clap softly, joining the dance.

A deer stumbles in, tripping over a root,
With an antlered bow, he hopes he looks cute.
Squirrels are gossiping, tails all ablaze,
About the latest trends in nut-collecting ways.

The wind whispers secrets, too funny to tell,
As branches entwine like they're under a spell.
Each crackling twig shares a funny riddle,
While critters all wiggle, their laughter middle.

In shadows that stretch, the night chaos reigns,
With laughter and mischief that only remains.
So gather your friends, let's share in the fun,
Under the starlit sky, the evening's begun!

The Forest's Gentle Farewell

As dusk descends, the forest holds sway,
With whispers and chuckles, it bids the day.
The brook giggles softly, making its way,
As crickets croon softly, 'Goodnight, hooray!'

Bears in pajamas, snoring in style,
While frogs in tuxedos sing every while.
The sunwaves goodbye in hues of delight,
As the laughing birches join in the night.

The wind tells a tale of fat pigeons' flights,
And fireflies twinkle like tiny bright knights.
Every tree grins with a gleam in its eye,
As the stars wink back from the velvet sky.

With a gentle bow, the forest takes leave,
In the humor of shadows, we all believe.
This whimsical world with its chuckles and glee,
Will always remain, wild and free!

A Palette of Purples and Greys

In hues of laughter, the sky starts to blend,
With purples and greys that the critters defend.
A moose in a beret strikes a pose for the show,
While chipmunks critique from the front row.

The clouds wear mustaches, puffy and bright,
As they giggle and tease, 'What a funny sight!'
The trees, all adorned in a foggy embrace,
Join in the laughter, setting the pace.

With every soft rustle, the night calls for jest,
'The squirrels are late to their nut-party fest!'
But who needs a plan when you've got such a view,
With colors of laughter painting the blue?

As shadows have fun in their playful ballet,
And the breeze whispers secrets of games they will play.
This palette of purples and greys, oh so bold,
Shapes tales of the forest, both silly and old.

A Serenade Beneath the Giants

In the shade of trees so grand,
Squirrels dance with acorn in hand,
A bear plays cards, what a sight,
While an owl hoots through the night.

Laughter echoes, the forest's cheer,
Rabbits gossip—a cheeky leer,
Frogs croak tunes from lily pads,
Even the breeze can't help but add.

Chipmunks juggle pine cones, oh my,
While fish in streams sing a lullaby,
Nature's circus, a wild delight,
As day winks out and bids goodnight.

With a hiccup, a raccoon takes a bow,
A porcupine looks on, "How did they allow?
Underneath these timbered frames,
We toast to life and silly games.

Evening's Caress Among the Cedars

Beneath the cedar, a party's on,
The sun dips low, but spirits are drawn,
A fox wears shades; he's quite the chap,
An owl takes selfies, a cheeky snap.

Bugs are buzzing in funky hats,
While deer join in for jig and chats,
Beetles tap dance on the leaves,
Creating rhythms that no one believes.

The sky paints pinks with a splash of blue,
While woodpeckers drum; what a hullabaloo,
The wind whispers secrets to ancient boughs,
And laughter erupts from wise old cows.

As stars peek out, the fun takes flight,
Creatures gather 'round, it's pure delight,
Among the cedars, joy does transpire,
Where silliness blooms like bright campfire.

The Fading Light Above the Pines

In a patch where shadows start to blend,
A raccoon walks a tightrope; oh, what a trend!
The sunset chuckles, feeling quite bold,
While pine needles share secrets untold.

Crickets chirp, forming a band,
A squirrel's the lead, with his nut in hand,
The flickering fireflies join in the fun,
Spinning in circles, under the sun.

Each animal dons a costume unique,
A porcupine's cape—now that's quite a peak!
The laughter spreads, a contagious glow,
Under the sigh of the pine trees low.

As the stars begin their shimmering show,
The whispers of night bring a playful flow,
With fading light, the antics abound,
In this jolly forest, laughter's the sound.

When Daylight Hugs the Horizon

When daylight snuggles, soft and close,
A skunk wears socks; it's quite morose,
A badger joins, clad in a tie,
While the sun waves a giggling goodbye.

The horizon blushes in shades of glee,
As creatures gather for the night spree,
Fireflies flash like a disco ball,
While ants form conga lines, having a ball.

With grins so wide, the critters unite,
Sharing tall tales of their daily fright,
A wise old turtle, slow and grand,
Chronicles the tales of every band.

As moonlight dances, casting its spell,
The forest whispers, "Oh, isn't it swell?
When daylight hugs with a wink and a tease,
Let's celebrate life, among the trees!

Nature's Nightriders in the Twilight

The squirrels in capes, take to the trees,
Zooming and darting, with the greatest of ease.
A raccoon in goggles, looking quite wise,
Chasing the fireflies, under darkening skies.

The owls are debating on branches so high,
Should they wear glasses, or just let it fly?
A playful racquetball rolled near their perch,
Causing a ruckus, it's quite the research!

A fox in a tux brushes his tail so bright,
Pretending to dance, it's a comical sight.
The beavers, they chuckle, while building their dam,
Hoping to catch a fish, or maybe a ham.

The shadows grow longer as laughter takes flight,
Through giggles and whispers, they welcome the night.
In the forest of fun, where mischief is grand,
The nature's nightriders joyfully stand.

Reverie of the Woodland Spirits

In the wee hours, the sprites start to play,
Spinning old tales, as they dance the night away.
Upon little mushrooms, they take their great leaps,
While the moon chuckles quietly, as the darkness peeps.

One sprite in a hat, much too big for his head,
Trips over a twig, falls right into bed!
A raccoon with a wink says, "Don't you despair,"
"There's plenty of room; just bring comfy chairs!"

The trees sway and giggle, their branches they toss,
As the pixies all cheer, "Who's the silliest boss?"
With the owls playing checkers 'neath stars up above,
It's a raucous affair filled with laughter and love.

As dawn starts to whisper, they scatter away,
Leaving behind tales of mischief and play.
In the reverie found, where magic does linger,
The woodland spirits wave with a cheeky finger.

The Gathering of the Evening Breeze

The evening breeze calls, with a whimsical grin,
Whispering secrets to the critters within.
The bunnies unite, with a twitch and a hop,
They plot their adventures, as day starts to stop.

A hedgehog, with mischief, dreams big and wide,
Wants to roll like a ball, on a fun, bumpy ride.
The owls hoot in laughter, their heads in a spin,
Challenging each other for who'll dive right in!

The crickets pull strings to a catchy old tune,
As the fireflies flicker, like tiny balloons.
All creatures assemble, for this grand little feast,
Where snacks are aplenty, and joy is released.

With a puff and a chuckle, the night shall unfold,
As stories are swapped, and legends retold.
In the gathering held with a wisecrack or two,
The evening breeze blows, with a giggle or two.

Hues of Nightfall on the Leaves

The sun dips low, in a splash of bold red,
Painting the leaves where the critters all tread.
The bunnies wear shades, as they strut on the ground,
Looking for carrots, but lost and quite browned.

A chipmunk in costume, complete with a tie,
Practices speeches, to the passing firefly.
"Let's throw a gala, at half-past the moon,
With sprouted grass salads and tunes from a raccoon!"

The leaves sway with laughter, as shadows collide,
With branches that wobble, like friends, side by side.
An owl gives a wink, "What a show we can bring,
When the stars start to yodel and crickets begin to sing."

In the hues of the night where the lantern bugs twirl,
The woodland's alive with a whimsical swirl.
From dusk until dawn, the adventure will weave,
In colors of laughter, oh, what we believe!

Glimmers Among the Elders

The old trees gossip with a creak,
Whispers of mischief, not so bleak.
They chuckle as squirrels chase their tails,
And share the secrets of their trails.

Beneath their branches, shadows dance,
While raccoons plot their next mischance.
Laughter echoes in the dusky air,
As owls wonder why they don't wear hair.

A deer trips over its own two feet,
While fireflies flash a personal beat.
The woodpecker laughs at the round young pups,
And everyone giggles as night comes up.

So here's to the elders, wise and sly,
With jokes so tall they might just fly.
In the glimmers, life's a funny show,
Under the trees where laughter flows.

Songs Carried By the Silent Wind

The breeze carries tunes of playful pranks,
As rabbits hop and waddle in ranks.
Each note is a giggle, a squeak, a cheer,
From the critters enjoying the evening's veneer.

Squirrels are hosting a dance-off tonight,
With moves that would cause even stars to ignite.
The shadows sway, a puppet on strings,
While the wind whistles louder, oh how it sings!

The moon joins in with a grin so wide,
As the fox attempts the cha-cha slide.
Crickets provide percussion, a lively beat,
To the comical rhythm of tiny feet.

With cada arpeggiato, the night unwinds,
And laughter spreads through the whispering pines.
These songs of mischief fill the air,
Under the cloak of night's jovial glare.

Constellations of Promise in the Shade

Stars above wink at the tales below,
As creatures gather for a light-hearted show.
A porcupine tries to juggle some leaves,
While the badger grins and quietly weaves.

The fireflies sparkle, a dance in mid-flight,
Their glow like laughter, oh what a sight!
Every twinkle tells of a prank gone awry,
As the night casts spells beneath a moonlit sky.

The shadows embrace the fun and the jest,
Each critter believes it's their time to fest.
Tales of bravery, oh what a delight,
As constellations cheer on the mischief tonight.

With every bright spark in the velvet black,
The forest chuckles, no sign to hold back.
In this realm of wonder, both low and high,
The promise of joy makes the stars ply.

Rustling Leaves and Fading Light

Leaves rustle secrets, giggling away,
While the sun bows down to end the day.
Chipmunks scamper in comedic haste,
As shadows stretch and begin to taste.

A lizard does a slow-motion slide,
While a raccoon covers its eyes with pride.
The evening chorus of quacks and peeps,
Makes the forest chuckle before it sleeps.

The twilight wraps around the green trees,
Where laughter is carried along with the breeze.
Every snap and twig bends toward the fun,
As night gathers close, and the day's done.

With each fading light, the humor grows,
In a world where giggles dance and glow.
So here's to the rustling, the playful plight,
In the fading shadows of fading light.

Secrets Murmured by the Brook

Bubbles giggle, stones all smile,
Fish tell tales of dreams worthwhile.
The frogs jump high, in leaps of glee,
While crickets laugh, so carelessly.

Squirrels gossip about their stash,
As ants march by, all in a flash.
The brook can't hold its chuckling cheer,
It spills its secrets, loud and clear.

Leaves sway gently, dance in rhyme,
While shadows play, in silly mime.
The willows bend, their heads in fun,
As night arrives, the games begun.

With every splash, a secret's spilled,
In this forest, laughter's thrilled.
Amid the sounds, a playful croak,
That sings the tales of joking folk.

A Veil of Night Among the Pines

The stars arrive, to take their seats,
While owls deliver nightly beats.
The pines stand tall, in cloaks of blue,
Swaying their branches, a dance anew.

The moonlight winks, as crickets croon,
And shadows play their silly tune.
A raccoon slips, all covered in mud,
While fireflies twinkle, like kids in a flood.

Bats zoom past, their speed unmatched,
While foxes laugh, all slyly scratched.
The breeze brings whispers of merry pranks,
As nature joins in on the fun-filled ranks.

Under the cloak of cozy night,
The woods erupt in pure delight.
Even the owls giggle on their perch,
In this woodland joke, there's nothing to lurch.

Beneath the Canopy's Embrace

Leaves whisper jokes, while branches sway,
The sun dips low, at the end of day.
A squirrel drops acorns, one by one,
Claiming it's storing, just for fun.

The shadows wink, in mischief's glow,
As butterflies dance, putting on a show.
While mushrooms sprout with tipsy flair,
Chortling softly, without a care.

The dappled light plays hide and seek,
As giggles echo from creek to peak.
A deer does a jig, so sprightly and quick,
Making the forest feel quite slick.

Under the canopy, laughter is found,
In every creature and every sound.
The joy of nature, in silly chime,
Becomes a moment, brilliantly prime.

The Quietude of Dimming Light

As daylight fades, the world in jest,
The woods hold stories, like a fest.
Bunnies hop in a playful line,
Trading secrets, feeling fine.

With each soft rustle, leaves join in,
As chipmunks chuckle, their cheeky grin.
A cloud floats by, wearing a hat,
A silly sight, imagine that!

Under the glow of a friendly star,
The owls recount, of places far.
And frogs perform their nightly play,
With grand applause at the end of the day.

The woods embrace the growing night,
With giggles echoing, full of delight.
As each creature wraps up their scheme,
They settle in, to let dreams beam.

Whispers of Dusk Among the Pines

The squirrels are now telling jokes,
As daylight wanes, they crack up folks.
A raccoon with a hat takes the stage,
Knocking over acorns like a wild rampage.

The owls laugh with their wise old eyes,
While fireflies buzz like tiny spies.
They gather round for a comedy show,
Under the stars where the breezes blow.

The trees sway, shaking their boughs,
Giggling softly as they take their bows.
Branches tickle the pines, quite absurd,
As nature thrives, joyfully unheard.

With laughter echoing through the wood,
Even the shadows join in for good.
And as night falls, the humor remains,
In this lively forest, where mirth reigns.

Shadows Embraced by the Forest Canopy

In the shade where the shadows dance,
A bear does a jig in a funny prance.
The hollering owls cheer him on,
While the trees roll their bark, 'til dawn.

Chipmunks sport hats of leafy green,
Strutting their stuff like a comedy scene.
They tell tales of nuts and their daring feats,
While the woodpecker drums out silly beats.

The toads croak a tune that's quite bizarre,
As frogs in tuxedos jump from afar.
A raccoon insists he can juggle fruit,
But he drops them all—oh, what a hoot!

And when the moon peeks through the leaves,
The laughter floats on the lightest eves.
In this wild woodland where gags unfold,
The forest secrets are funny, not old.

The Evening Song of the Cedar Grove

Cedar trees hum a lively tune,
As crickets pull up to play by the moon.
A fox in a scarf joins the fun parade,
While a badger's hopping in the shade.

Gather round, here comes the bard,
A porcupine strumming a makeshift guitar.
He sings of adventures, wild and silly,
While the moonlight bathes the grove, oh so frilly.

Squirrels mimic all the great shows,
Acting like humans, striking funny poses.
As shadows stretch in a comedic twist,
They compete for the crown of the silliest mist.

With giggles and snorts filling the air,
The cedar grove sparkles with joyous flair.
Oh, what a sight, this merry brigade,
As night wraps around their jester parade.

Flickering Light Beneath the Canopy

Underneath the stars, a flicker shines,
A raccoon in shades draws funny lines.
As fireflies zip to light the night,
His stand-up routine takes a bright flight.

The bears are chuckling, rolling in moss,
In a game of charades, they'll be the boss.
"Catch the fish!" one yells, with a comical flair,
While the trees play along, just standing there.

The wind stirs up stories from long ago,
Of a moose who wore mismatched bows.
He tripped on a branch, fell into a stream,
But laugh as we might, he still reigns supreme.

As the night deepens, the giggles grow loud,
Creating a concert, oh, we're all so proud.
A forest of laughter, where shadows ignite,
In this quirky place, everybody's all right.

www.ingramcontent.com/pod-product-compliance
Lightning Source LLC
Chambersburg PA
CBHW071838160426
43209CB00003B/340